So You Think You Want to Follow Christ? Study Guide

Written by Steven E Lindsey
Illustrated/Design Layout by Jan Asleson

Copywrite © 2023 Steven E Lindsey

All rights reserved. No part of this book may be reproduced in any form or by any electronic or mechanical means including information storage and retrieval systems, without permission in writing from the publisher, except by reviewers, who may quote brief passages in review...

ISBN 9798218141851

Library of Congress Control Number 2023901162

THE HOLY BIBLE, NEW INTERNATIONAL VERSION®, NIV® Copyright © 1973, 1978, 1984, 2011 by Biblica, Inc. Used by permission. All rights reserved worldwide.

Printed in the United States of America by Ingram Spark/Lightning Source

Published by Spirit Wings Designs 2023
daslpacker55@yahoo.com

Visit me at www.spiritwingsdesigns.com

So You Think You Want to Follow Christ?

Study Guide

Written
by
Steven E Lindsey

Illustrated by Jan Asleson

Acknowledgements

As the author I have sought the collaboration and knowledge of many to be certain this study guide is factual and consistent with the Bible. I want to thank our Men's Study Group with whom I regularly meet. Jan Asleson, who did the illustrations and her husband David. Pastor Nick Grimm who encourages me. Also, my wife Priscilla and all those who have supported me along the way and helped me find a life following Jesus.

This Book Is Dedicated to:

My Mother who read Hulbert's Bible Stories to me as a child, my Grandmother who taught my High School Sunday School Class, my Father who showed me how Christians are to live, my wife Priscilla, who has shown me what unconditional love can be, standing by me daily, and to Jesus Christ, my Savior.

Forward

This study is intended to give concept and reason to your desire for a deeper more intimate relationship with Christ. It raises questions but allows the reader to find the answers on how to respond to Christ's calling. Further, it reveals the blessings God has prepared for His believers. I hope to convey the idea that becoming a Christian is a life-long journey. And, "that you walk worthy of God, who is calling you to His Kingdom and Glory." 1 Thessalonians 2:12

So You Think You Want to Follow Christ? Study Guide

I. Who is Jesus?

    Creation, Prophesy, Trinity, God's Word, Covenants

II. What is the Gospel Message?

    Life and Character of Jesus, Grace, Faith, Love Commands

III. Living Like Jesus

    Believe, Repent, Baptize, Lord's Supper, Giving, Prayer, Fellowship Discipleship etc.

IV. Expectations / Rewards.

    Peace, Support, Grace, Salvation

Introduction

This study guide is designed to complement "So You Think You Want to Follow Christ?" authored By Steven E Lindsey, and illustrated by Jan Asleson. It is designed to help new Christians or those contemplating the decision to follow Jesus Christ. I hope to introduce you to the Gospel Message and offer an insight to Christ's Calling. You will need a Bible to complete this study. The Bible is invaluable in your quest to follow Jesus. The purpose for the book and study guide is to expose that following Jesus is not particularly an emotional decision but a deliberate act with intention of a lifelong journey. I wish you success in your journey and many blessings along the way as you approach your destination.

1. Who is Jesus?

Why would I follow Jesus?

C. S. Lewis, a prominent British Theologian, states, *"Here begins our division of a Christian and mere people. This man, Jesus, is either the Son of God or He is a mad lunatic or the most amazing magician to ever walk the earth. The choice is yours. Was He a fool, a demon, or is He what He claims, the Son of God"*

Let us begin our quest with the Bible. The Bible is a collection of letters and manuscripts written by men who were inspired by God. Many of the documents are hundreds, if not thousands, years old and have been preserved for centuries. It was divided into Chapters and Verses later in history to allow for reference to specific texts. There are additional documents and letters written but were not included in what we call the Bible today. The Bible has been translated from the original Hebrew and Greek to nearly every language known being very careful not to alter or change its initial meaning. Similarly, it has been rewritten into several dialects to make it more easily understood. Care has been made to not change the meaning or to mislead the reader. In studying the Bible, it is often good to study a different dialect or to refer to the original Hebrew or Greek Message.

At some point in coming to a decision to follow Jesus, we must have faith and believe. Paul, who was chosen by God to introduce Jesus' Gospel to the world, states that we are saved by faith through the grace of God by Jesus Christ. What is faith? Webster defines faith as "the unquestioning belief that does not require proof of existence or the evidence thereof."

Hebrews 11:1 states, "faith is confidence in what we hope for and assurance about what we do not yet see." Could it be that faith is the most important concept in our search for Jesus? It is clearly where the promise of God is made real to His redeemed. We who are saved and follow Jesus are not without evidence. First, there is the Bible as we have already discussed. Secondly, there is creation. The complexity in the design of creation speaks for itself. The order of the universe speaks volumes. God made the universe so precise that consistent formulas can define and predict the stars' and planets' positions and paths. This world is wonderfully made and totally beyond happenstance and chance. Romans 1:20, "For since the creation of the world, God's invisible qualities; His eternal power and divine nature; have been clearly seen, being understood from what has been made, so that people are without excuse." Your faith need not be either blind or uncertain. Herein is the certainty we can enjoy by faith and the surety of all we can hope for.

Who, then, is Jesus?

The Bible has many accounts of Jesus written by witnesses to His life on earth. Further, the Bible tells us of Jesus before He was born to our earth. There are prophecies hundreds of years before His birth, telling of his coming and cheering the expectation of His arrival. Jesus is God's Son and is the focal point of the entire Bible, both Old and New Testaments. The first four Books of the New Testament record Jesus' life on earth while the remainder of the New Testament helps us understand how we are to worship Jesus and live our lives as examples. It tells us of His resurrection, witnessed by hundreds, and His ascension to Heaven. It is important to study Jesus' life and read these letters so we can grow in faith. We grow in faith by hearing and reading God's Word. This is how we can follow Jesus, by following His example.

Is Jesus Who He Says?

To learn who Jesus is and learn to believe He exists (faith) and know we want to follow Him we must study and learn. The Old Testament sets the stage for the coming of Jesus. Even His death on the cross was foretold (Psalm 22:16-18) nearly 1,000 years before His birth. This was before execution on a cross was practiced. Circumstances of His birthplace, lineage, and death were foretold. Jesus stands as evidence to the prophecies of His Kingdom. As many as forty-seven messianic predictions in the Old Testament are clearly fulfilled in Jesus' life. This was not and could not have been happenstance. Jesus is real. Genesis 3:15, 12:3, 22:18, 17:19, 2;12, 49:10, Micah 5:2, Isaiah 6:9-10, 7:14, 11:1, 9:1-2, 40:35, 53:3 Numbers 24:17, 2 Samuel 7:12-13, Hosea 11:1, Jeremiah 3:15, Malachi 3:1,4:5-6, Psalm 2:7, 69:8, 78:2-4, Deuteronomy 18:15, and many more scriptures predicted the coming Christ. For reference, read "Old Testament Prophecies of Jesus", by Mary Fairchild.

Collectively these prophecies and their fulfillment are absolute proof of Christ's deity. It is further used to confirm His claim to be the Son of God to whom God gave full authority of all things, thus establishing his Kingdom. Jesus explains His fulfillment of these prophecies. (Luke 24:25-27). There is no question that Jesus Christ, the King, was born by immaculate conception, was baptized, anointed Christ by God, served God on earth as in heaven, was crucified, dead and buried, and raised from the dead as witnessed by hundreds. He then ascended into heaven where he prepares a place for us. Amen! (Colossians 1:15-24)

Discussion:

1. What are Jesus' commands for when we believe, repent and are baptized? Matthew 28:18-20.

2. What does Jesus say to do when we decide to follow Him? Romans 10:9-10, Acts 2:38, 1 Peter 3:18-22.

3. Why did John write his gospel message? John 20:30-31

4. Who is John referring to as the "Word" in John 1:1?

5. Why is it so important to preserve the Bible text in exact form and purpose? Revelations 22:19-21.

6. Why do we need the Lord? Judges 21:25, 18:1, 19:1.

7. Faith is our foundation of belief:
    - S_____ by faith. Eph 2:8-9
    - L_____ by faith Rm 1:17.
    - Received R_____ by faith Rm 4:13
    - J_____ by faith Rm 5:1.
    - Receive G_____ by faith Eph 2:8
    - Receive H_____ S_____ Gal 3:14
    - B_____ by faith. Gal 3:9'

8. What are the evidences of my faith that others can see in me?

9. What is faith in Jesus? Hebrews 11, Gal 2:16, Eph 2:8.

10. Is my faith growing and what kind of example am I for my family, at work, in my community?

II. What is the Gospel?

Jesus clearly defines the Gospel Message in Matthew 28:18-20. The gospel is the life and character of Jesus Christ. He commands that we are to Repent, Believe and Follow Him. We are to be obedient to His example and commands. We are to emulate His very character. We must believe that He died and was buried as a sacrifice to forgive our sins, once for all. Further, we must believe He rose from the grave as witnessed by many and ascended to Heaven where he prepares a place for us. Hebrews 4:14. Very simply this is the Gospel Message. Paul expands on it in Acts 2.

All this Jesus summarizes as: "Love." "Love the Lord your God with all your heart and soul. Love your neighbor as yourself. Go and make disciples of all peoples baptizing in the name of the Father, Son and the Holy Spirit." Teach the people to obey the commands of Jesus, and Jesus will be with you forever. Love is a consistent theme throughout the whole Bible: Old and New Testaments. Love God, Love yourself, your neighbor and God's creation. Matthew 22:36-38.

In loving God, we love the Son and the Spirit, referred to as the Trinity. Three in one. Though three distinct beings having individual characteristics, they act as one body. One can think of the Trinity like marriage. Marriage is between a husband and wife, two people, who act as one. One goal, One thought, One union – singular but multiple. Of one mind.

Perhaps loving one's self requires further explanation. God desires to be with man. He desires an intimate relationship. He walked and spoke directly to Adam in the Garden of Eden. He loves His creation and wanted to have a personal companionship with man. He still does. But, sin and evil, which God detests, entered the world. God chose to separate Himself from sinful man because of it. Adam and Eve were left separated from God and the Garden.

God soon instructed Moses to build the tabernacle. God designed it and instructed Moses as to its construction. There was one room, the Holy of Holies, that only the priest could enter at special times. The Holy of Holies was separated from the remainder of the Tabernacle by a huge heavy curtain. This was where God lived. Close to His creation, again. The Ark of the Covenant was constructed at God's instruction so He could travel with His people. Special people were selected to carry the ark and to manage the Tabernacle. God was with His people. But the people continued to sin.

Finally, because of His love for Mankind and His desire for an intimate relationship with man, He sent Jesus, Christ. He sent Jesus to be an example but more than that God sent Jesus to be a "Once for All" sacrifice for the forgiveness of sin to whomever would BELIEVE, REPENT AND FOLLOW JESUS.

In the age of man between Adam and Jesus, God required blood sacrifice for the forgiveness of sin. Sacrifice of the first and best, often a lamb. Jesus became God's ultimate sacrifice once for all of mankind. Jesus, though innocent and blameless, (like a lamb) was put to death. God's Son, to atone for the sins of the world. He was crucified, dead and buried. But, on the third day, He was raised from the dead, proving God's power over death and His promise (covenant) of Salvation for all who believe and choose to follow Christ.

When Jesus died on the cross, there was an earthquake and the curtain that separated the Tabernacle was ripped top to bottom, exposing the Holy of Holies forever. At this time, Man becomes God's Temple. The Holy Spirit now resides in Man with the destruction of the Tabernacle. No more blood offerings, Christ is our sacrifice, died in our place once for all. For those who believe, repent, and are baptized, we are God's Temple. The Spirit of God lives in you and will lead you, if you allow. You are the Temple. This is a major reason we are to love ourselves and our neighbor. 1 Corinthians 6:19.

By following Jesus, obeying His commands, discipling people to God, God extends His grace for Salvation. In all likelihood, even though we have the best of intensions, we will sin, but that was why Jesus died. Not so that we could continue to sin but rather, when we slip or fail. Jesus' sacrifice for the forgiveness of sin suffices as we trust in the Spirit and follow Jesus. It is therefore imperative that we keep God's Temple presentable for Him and make concerted effort to sin no more.

In keeping ourselves presentable and able to disciple and teach others as commanded, we must study and learn the gospel message. We grow in faith through hearing and study. We learn by studying Bible scriptures and fellowship with fellow Christians. Christ states we are saved by our faith. So, to present ourselves to God and disciple to the world we must grow in our faith. We must learn. We learn through reading, preaching, and teaching. John 14:23.

Further, we are to follow Jesus' commands and explain them to others. In Matthew 28:18, God gave all authority to Jesus Christ, the King. As King, King of our lives, we serve and worship Him while obeying His commands. John 13:34. Believe, Repent, Baptize, Pray, Disciple, Love, give generously, Fellowship, Grow in Faith, and share the Lord's Supper to remember Christs sacrifice. These are most of Christ's commands but of all these Love is the most important. 1 Corinthians 13:13.

Discussion:

1. Jesus is called Immanuel. What does Immanuel mean and how does it relate to the gospel message? Matthew 1:23, Isaiah 7:14.

2. How does Jesus mean for us to love our neighbor as ourselves? Just who is our neighbor? Mark 12:28-34, Luke 10: 29-37.

3. How can you grow your faith in Jesus? Hebrews 11:6. Mark 11:22-24, James 2:14-23, Romans 10:17, Ephesians 3:20.

4. Why should you know the Gospel Message? Romans 10:17

5. Once we have accepted Christ what do we do? Matthew 28:18-20, 2 Timothy 1:14.

6. Do you as a new believer have a different insight to living than you have had previously? 1 Corinthians 1:20, 2:14, 13:16.

111. Living Like Jesus

"How Do I Respond?"

Believe:

When we decide to follow Jesus, how and what are we to do? Jesus, Himself, says first we are to believe. To believe we need to recognize Jesus as God's Son, God as Father, and the Holy Spirit. We must believe God to be the Master Architect and Creator of all things. We must believe we are a part of God's creation and God made each of us special and unique with a purpose in His Kingdom. We need to believe that Jesus willingly died on the cross, was buried once for all to forgive our sins and fulfill scripture, and was raised from the dead promising salvation to all believers, and rose to Heaven preparing a place for us.

We need to believe that we are God's temple and that the Holy Spirit resides in us to guide us in life, Christ says to believe and we will never perish (John 3:15-18) But our belief demands faith. We place our faith in the gospel message with the assurance that God will reward us with grace in righteousness through Jesus Christ and that we ultimately receive salvation through the forgiveness of sin. Hebrews 11:1 "it is by grace you are saved by faith and salvation is His gift of grace poured into our soul by the Holy Spirit." Ephesians 28:9.

Repent:

Repentance is much more than just being sorry. Repentance is remorse and a sincere desire to change. It is the recognition that our prior life and actions are in opposition to following Jesus and what he would have us do. To live like Jesus, we have to change direction. Change our lives completely. It will likely mean we need to change our friends and how we value the things we do, and who we do things with.

Repentance brings about a desire to change our habits and stop sinning. We will falter and slip because we are human but that is where we can depend on the Holy Spirit. As we strive to move away from those things that are sinful we can pray that the Spirit will give us strength to turn away, Sometimes it is difficult because Satan loves to spoil Christians. It is important you carefully choose activities and fellowship as new believers. Cultivate your life to avoid the pitfalls of your prior life and it will become easier. Pray the Holy Spirit will assist you and remove the temptation. Satan tempted Jesus, too. Matthew 4:1-18. He tempts every Christian. How we meet that temptation defines how much we grow in faith. Repentance is necessary every time we fail. God will forgive us as long as we believe and we will fail less often if we will just repent.

Baptize:

We are to be baptized as soon as we believe and repent. Jesus was our example and was baptized to become the reason we are now baptized. Baptism is Greek for immerse. It is expressive symbolism of the death, burial, and resurrection of Jesus Christ. Death to an old way of life, buried, arising into newness of life, being "Born Again." It is an outward expression of a change of heart and life. It is a personal, voluntary decision by a knowing individual to follow Jesus and confirm their belief in the gospel message. Acts 2:38-41. There is no other way.

The Holy Spirit came upon Jesus in the bodily form of a dove as John the Baptist baptized Him. Here God introduces Jesus to His ministry when God said," This is my Son with whom I am well pleased." There are scriptures that would suggest the Holy Spirit enters the believer at baptism. However, Acts 10 suggests, we gentiles receive the Spirit prior to baptism immediately upon believing. Galatians 3:2. The exact time the Spirit enters a Christian can be needlessly argued but the fact remains that the Spirit resides in God's temple; You. Further, baptism is a command and is a necessary act in our quest to follow Jesus. Baptism sets us apart from the world and through the help of the Holy Spirit gives us strength to combat the pressures and temptations of a sin filled world and Satan. Acts 18:24-26, 19:1-7.

Following Jesus and learning to live like Jesus requires several other expectations: Sharing the Lord's Supper, fellowship, generosity in giving, prayer and discipleship. These are commands Jesus spoke of and examples we are to live by.

The Lord's Supper:

The Lord's supper was when Jesus shared the Feast of the Passover with his disciples in the upper room. It is where he exposed Judas Iscariot for betraying Him. This was just prior to His execution. He took the bread and broke it saying, "Take, eat, this is my body." Then He took the cup of new wine, gave thanks, and said, "This is my blood of the New Covenant, which is shed for many." Mark 14:22-25. "Do this to remember Me." John 6:53-59. The bread and juice symbolize the body and blood of the sacrifice, sealing the covenant between God and man. Jesus' death on the cross was for the forgiveness of sin. (Luke 22:18-22).

Initially Christians called this ceremony "thanksgiving" though today we call it communion. Many churches disagree on the frequency to observe but it should be frequent and sacred. Treat communion as a memorial to the, once for all time, sacrifice by Jesus. It is not a re-sacrifice (Hebrews 10:12) but is a serious moment we set aside to remember and cherish the gospel message and ask Christ to forgive us as we fall short of perfection in many ways.

"But when this Priest had offered the one supreme sacrifice for sin for all time He sat down on a throne at the right hand of God, waiting until all His whispering enemies are subdued and turn into His footstool." Hebrews 10:12

Fellowship:

Fellowship is not particularly a command. But Jesus warns us to avoid continued fellowship with unbelievers, and leads us to understand that in our new lives in Christ righteousness and wickedness have nothing in common. By fellowship we can have mutual support. We meet together as Christians to support our fellow believers but often become the supported. In growing our faith through hearing, fellowship is necessary. Romans 10:17. Sharing our confession of faith is also important in growing in faith while following Jesus. Ephesians 4:16.

"So faith comes from hearing, and hearing through the word of Christ." Romans 10:17

"From Him the whole body, joined and held together by every supporting ligament, grows and builds itself up in love, as each part does its work." Ephesians 4:16

Giving and Tithe:

Tithe in the Old Testament is a command. The absence of tithe was considered robbing God (Malachi 3:8). Tithe was considered ten percent. (Nehemiah 10:38). It was a gift as important as the sacrifice and was brought to the storeroom of the tabernacle as grain, new wine, olive oil, etc. (Nehemiah 13:12). The tithe was to support the priests and Levites whom God had appointed to manage the Tabernacle or Temple.

Today we continue this in giving, though not a command of measure. Christ commands us to give what you can. Give from your heart, not reluctantly or under compulsion, for God loves the cheerful giver. Jesus says God will bless those who give abundantly and meet the Church's needs. Love is the format for giving to God's Kingdom. Christ simply says to give and it will be given you. Give a good measure. For with what you measure, it will be measured to you. Luke 6:38. Fellowship and Giving are an expectation that rewards the giver more that the gift. Perhaps 10 percent could be considered a good beginning but Jesus simply says to give as you can.

Discipleship:

Christ was specific about discipleship. Just prior to His ascension following the resurrection, he said to go into all nations, to all peoples, baptizing in the name of the Father, Son and Holy Spirit teaching all the things He commanded. Our charge is NOT to keep the gospel message secret but spread it to the ends of the earth. We are to Go. We are to share what we know to be true with our family, those with whom we work and those we come in contact with. Share the gospel message as we learn it, do not wait. Avoid arguments and teach with love and humility. Do not be arrogant or demanding just share what you know. Invite people to learn with you. Study and share together as you grow in faith. Invite those you meet to join you in Following Jesus.

Discussion:

1. Can you explain the difference in baptism by John the Baptist and that of the apostles and today? Acts 19.

2. What does "once for all" mean when referring to Christ's death on the cross? Hebrews 7:27, 10:1.

3. How are you saved? Ephesians 2:8-9, Acts 13:39.

4. Not by works. Does this mean we are to simply come to church and sit in a pew? Matthew 28:18-20, Galatians 3:2-3.

5. Why is prayer important? Ephesians 6:18.

6. Why should you be baptized? Mat 28:18-29, Acts 2:37-41, 8:38-39, John 3:23, Mark 1:15

Expectations / Rewards

"Blessings to Expect"

Once we believe, repent and are baptized, the New Testament (Covenant) promises reward for serving the King Jesus. These are basically Peace, Support, Grace, and Salvation; ultimately righteousness through Jesus Christ. God's love for his creation and desire for an intimate relationship rewards our devotion and worship with all these fruits of the Spirit. Gal 5:22. There is peace with our lives as we gain the assurance that we are forgiven and no longer have the debt of sin upon us. We have the assurance that Christ did die for our sins and that we can be found righteous in God's eyes through Christ. Matt 6:33, Rom 6:16

There is also the assurance of having the Holy Spirit. (Romans 14:17) God delivers the Holy Spirit to all who believe. (Acts 2:38). The Holy Spirit gives us daily support in life's struggles. It will give us words when we need them in God's name. (Acts 4: 25) The Spirit gives us strength to repel Satan. The support of the Spirit and the fellowship of our Church family is invaluable in living our lives pleasing to Christ; Following Jesus.

Grace:

Grace, next to love is one of the most important concepts of following Jesus. It is clearly expressed in the promises of Scripture. Grace is the result of God's love for His creation even though that gift is so unmerited. (Romans 3:23). Another term for grace is mercy. We lived in a world where without Jesus we would get what we deserve, the results of judgement. Paul tells us, "The grace of God has appeared, bringing salvation for all people, training us to renounce ungodliness and worldly passions, and live self-controlled upright, and godly lives." (Titus 2:11) Spiritual growth does not just happen overnight; we must "grow in the grace and knowledge of our savior Jesus Christ (2 Peter 2:18) God chooses mercy… grace.

Salvation:

The cross at Calvary fulfilled God's plan for the salvation of the world. It is the end reward, the gift of grace by God for following Jesus. Becoming a Christian does not just happen, it is a process. It is the remainder of your life. Salvation is when we meet Christ. It reflects the covenant (promise) that if we believe, repent, and are baptized and obey Christ's commands we can fully expect to join Jesus when we die. Romans 11:16. God says we are saved by faith through grace by Jesus Christ, never on our own merit. Ephesians 2:8-9.

Prayer:

Prayer is the opportunity we have been given to communicate directly with God, His Son, and the Spirit. Jesus set aside time to pray and speak to His Father even though He himself was deity. (Luke 5:15). He used prayer to recharge himself when He needed strength. We should follow His example. We need prayer to face the challenges of daily life. When we become distracted, we can use prayer to refocus and seek strength and purpose with Christ through His Spirit. Christ gave us an example of how to pray in Matthew 6:9-13. However, we really need no primer, God listens if we ask in Jesus' Holy name and sincerely believe. Pray with a thankful heart and ask that God's will be done. He already knows our needs but if a need is heavy on your heart, ask God to deliver. Then, be patient. Nothing is too large or too small for God, always ask for His will be done because only He knows the bigger picture in life. James 5:16 reminds us that if we desire our prayers to be answered, we need our hearts right with God, so do ask Him to forgive you. Do not hesitate to pray. Set aside a time, daily, that you devote to prayer. Prayer is also where we can worship and praise our Lord and Savior.

This study is only the beginning of a lifetime Following Jesus. There is much more to be found in the Bible. Every time we read the Bible, God reveals more truths and understanding. There is always more one can do to feel the full presence of the Lord in our life. But, live life like Jesus. May your journey to salvation be one of joy and sharing. Amen.

Discussion:

1. Why is it important to attend church regularly and become involved in it? 1 Corinthians 12:12-14.

2. How do we pray? Heb 1:1-5. Eph 5:20, Romans 8:26, Mat 6:5-15, John 15:16, 16:23, Jude 20

3. When does the Holy Spirit become a part of you: Eph 1:13-14.

4. How are you, a gentile, affected by the law expressed throughout the Old Testament?

    Romans 3:21-22, 1 Tim 1:3-7, Col 2:3, Col 2:16-23 Galatians 3:11

5. How can we show grace in our lives? 1 Peter 4:16

6. What is salvation by faith? Eph 2:4-9, Romans 2:24

Steven E Lindsey
Author

Steven E Lindsey is retired in southeast Kansas. He and wife, Priscilla, have bred, raised, trained and ridden Arabian horses for over forty years for distance events. They have seen a great deal of God's creation from between horses' ears. Steve was a forester professionally, though later in life he worked in the insurance industry as agent, owner, and wholesaler. They have served at several churches in Kansas, Colorado, and Missouri, and are now part of the leadership in a newer plant, Impact Christian Church in Independence, Kansas. Not a pastor, not a priest. Just one of God's servants waiting to join Him in the Kingdom.

You can contact Steve at: lindseyagency@yahoo.com

 Jan Asleson - Author/Illustrator

My designs are inspired by a desire to share with others the beauty of God's creation that I see around me. My passion is to encourage others through my artistic mediums to not give up on their dreams, to recognize the Blessings all around them and to know that there is always hope.

I find my creativity in many mediums including watercolor, acrylics, pastels, oils, jewelry design, book illustration work, silk art, metal work, watercolor and portraiture.

I live in South-East Kansas with my husband David.

You can find me at www.spiritwingsdesigns.com

www.ingramcontent.com/pod-product-compliance
Lightning Source LLC
LaVergne TN
LVHW072124060526
838201LV00069B/4970